ALAIN BEROF

GAME OF LIFE

The Ultimate Guide to Living The Life You Want, Discover the Secrets and Useful Tips on How You Can Live The Live You Know You Deserve

Descrierea CIP a Bibliotecii Naționale a României
ALAIN BEROF
   GAME OF LIFE. The Ultimate Guide to Living The Life You Want, Discover the Secrets and Useful Tips on How You Can Live The Live You Know You Deserve / Alain Berof. – Bucharest: Editura My Ebook, 2020
   ISBN 978-606-983-598-2

ALAIN BEROF

GAME OF LIFE

The Ultimate Guide to Living The Life You Want, Discover the Secrets and Useful Tips on How You Can Live The Live You Know You Deserve

My Ebook Publishing House
Bucharest, 2020

TABLE OF CONTENTS

Foreword

The buzz about abundance is spreading just like wildfire. And it is about time that you need to wake up and have a deeper understanding about yourself and about who you truly are. In addition to that, you should also be aware about what you're capable of doing and learn about the limitless resources that are available out there. Get all the info you need here.

Live The Life You Know You Deserve

CHAPTER 1

INTRODUCTION

Synopsis

You are actually a three dimensional being, and it's a sad fact that most people have limited beliefs, spending their lives not knowing this fact. It's not too late for your to realize that there's more in life than all the material things, the skin, bones, and meat that you see. It is time for you to know that you can truly begin living your life in a much broader perspective.

The Basics

There's an amazing inner world existing beyond what you can actually see with your eyes. This world contains all essential things such as resources, power, wealth, and the real meaning of your existence. It is a work that allows you to live your life fully, live large, do and be anything you want. The problem is that this line seems very common but in fact lots of people are unaware of it. But most people are trying to thrive into this world with the use of the 5 senses that you originally use in growing.

Your external senses – touching hearing, smelling, tasting, and seeing are extremely essential but these mustn't be used in order to govern your life. Contrary to the belief, these five senses aren't the most extraordinary and powerful asset. Well, each creature is given a gift of external senses and since you are God's creation, you need to begin using your real given gifts rather than use the simplest form of expressions that almost all existing creatures have.

But this is actually where the real problem lies, because while most teachers of total development and self growth tell you about creating wealth and abundance, they don't potentially teach you the real meaning of creating wealth. You probably heard about using your mind, and for a fact it is true. But while it is true, you still don't know how exactly you can use your mind.

First and foremost, you should understand that developing abundance in life is an excellent skill set, which you should learn and remind yourself with in order for you to have abundance flowing right into your life. Lots of people do believe that they are operating in 3 levels of essential awareness simultaneously. And that their highest form would be their soul or spirit level, which is your connection and extension to source your needed energy. When it becomes your truth, then you will begin to discover and realize that you need to actually operate from your highest potential. With this, you'll see that abundance is really a skill which you need to learn.

With your current programming and upbringing, you have neglected to connect with the higher plane, which will help you guide your creative forces and energies that you inherently possess. Thus, your should first learn the skill of creating abundance, make it a dance of your life, and by this you are opening the flood gate of riches, wealth, and prosperity into your daily lives.

CHAPTER 2

FIGURING OUT WHAT ABUNDANCE
MEANS TO YOU

Synopsis

What does abundance really means to you? You hear this word a lot but have you ever really thought about what 'true' abundance and wealth really is? And most importantly how you may experience more from it in life? Do you believe that abundance and wealth is possible for the different aspect of your life? The answers to these questions will be revealed by simply identifying and observing what is currently going on with the different facets of your own life – financially, physically, emotionally, and spiritually.

What Is It

Although lots of people claim of having an exceptionally good life, this determination is often made from the traditionally taught and established perceptions and beliefs taught to you and are held by you, based on limited understanding about what 'Good Life' really means and about the limitless resources that are available for anyone who are willing to thrive deeply enough in order to discover the real meaning of it.

In reality, the achievement of abundance and real wealth is infinite in nature but is equally available for anyone willing to identify and enhance their skills and ability to start choosing whatever it is that they prefer to experience. And yes, you are not an exception. As you will discover you source, whatever you perceive it to be, it consists of limitless supply for whatever you prefer to experience in life provided that you choose to believe and conceive that you can and it will. Sadly, lots of people make choices unconsciously; they never understand why they're unable to have that abundance, harmony, and fulfillment in life.

Why not ask yourself with these questions?

- Are you having true happiness and abundance in life?
- Do you love your work and find it financially rewarding and fulfilling?
- Are you having enough time for you to do the things you love the most?
- Do you really have sufficient money for you to do all the things you want?
- Are you enjoying wholesome, deeply satisfying, and fulfilling relationships?
- Are you having a vigorous and vivacious physical health?
- Are your heartfelt dreams as well as you wants fulfilled in the different aspect of life?

If your answer to these questions is NO, then you're not enjoying and experiencing a quality of life that everyone is capable of having.

Abundance and wealth means different things from different people. For some, abundance may be identified as having lots of money. And based on others' perspective and beliefs, it may actually mean something absolutely different.

16

Although enough financial resources means a lot to people since it is a very essential facet of abundance and wealth in today's generation, but money only makes up a tiny portion from the entire equation when it comes to 'Real Abundance'. Unless all the other essential aspects of your life are aligned harmoniously, the experience of real abundance and the fulfillment that is available will elude you continually and it will appear to be impossible and unattainable.

Lasting and true abundance and wealth will result from a perfect balance in the fundamental areas of your life.

CHAPTER 3

DECIDING WHAT YOU ARE LACKING

Synopsis

Regardless of your age, whether you're in your 30's or 60's, all people have questions and doubt about their life's direction. You may feel bored, busy with lots of projects, feeling empty romantically, you may feel depressed because of you job and feel that it's a dead end, and you may even feel trapped in a certain situation like family drama, kids, or marriage.

There are actually lots of people who busy themselves by having mundane projects and works in order to provide a purpose to their life, but most of them are unhappy and unsatisfied. They're just passing their time, giving themselves with something to perceive as essential. At least these people are trying, though.

Have A Look

Every person needs to feel something. You need to have that feeling of making a huge difference, from time to time. Some people are quite restless, the reason why they give themselves a lot of projects. It definitely gives them something FRESH and NEW to learn and discover, allowing them to keep on learning and growing and never become stagnant.

Well, there is a reason why you feel like there is something lacking in your life. It is you heart, body, and mind that lets you know and feel that you're not complete. You feel its lack of purpose and passion.

Without natural purpose and passion, you may start to feel that emptiness. The projects and activities that you engage yourself in may seem just routines that you are on an autopilot. Time passes by, you feel like nothing of great value and essence is being achieved and accomplished in your life.

Areas that you may have missing pieces:

- Meaningful work
- Social life
- Use of your skills
- Relationships

- Finances
- Fitness
- Love
- Health
- Spirituality

Regaining your real passion in life as well as that essential feeling that you everything you do in life actually has meaning, is important for your fulfillment and real happiness. If you need to suppress yourself because of so many boundaries, you need some adjusting to do in order for you to allow and let more freedom and flexibility flow in your life.

If you've so much time available on your hand, which is the dilemma of so many people, it can also feel extremely depressing. You won't feel worthy at all, as you're not utilizing your time to do something essential in a more valuable way. What people are actually missing in life in not all external things, but internal.

It is often an emotion of feeling that's not being achieved or met. To simply put it, you are the obstacle that hinders yourself from being happy, or feeling that you are missing or lacking something – this is so because you are the one who is in charge of your life. When you identify the things that you are lacking, discover the missing pieces to appreciate that things you have accomplished, and all the things you own, then you can now focus on filling the gaps.

CHAPTER 4

HOW ABUNDANCE WORKS

Synopsis

Are you having problems about your finances? Do you often feel that you aren't experiencing real success that you want in life?

If so, you should establish an absolute and strong connection and relationship with your 'higher self' – your 'true self'. With this, you will automatically experience better and more success and abundance in life. Your 'higher self' is the 'real you', and its nature is real abundance. Your 'higher self' is connected with a stream of success and abundance as well as with the light that flows constantly from the spirit/universal. But the dilemma with so many people is that they considerably narrow down the path where abundance flows into their lives. And this is so because of their limiting and false beliefs and perceptions, negative momentums, bad habits, etc. When you take the essential steps of reuniting with your higher self, you will be able to find the abundance valve is opening bigger and bigger allowing more and more abundance to flow into life!

The Abundance Channel

In order to have a much better visualization of that abundance energy stream, which constantly pours from the 'universal' through your 'higher self' consider it as a huge golden channel that offers radiant energy fully flowing into your life. Eliminate all limiting and false beliefs, your false perceptions, negative energies, and limiting thoughts that you have engaged yourself in. They don't only limit the abundance flow in life, but they also hinders your connection with the real you.

Increase The Flow Of Success And Abundance In Life

If you discover and do something to overcome all the limiting beliefs, negative momentums, and bad habits, you'll be able to strip yourself away from all the things that hinder abundance to flow into your life. In addition to that, cultivating your positive momentums such as peace, harmony, and joy will

23

further and better dissolve more negativity and will strengthen and enhance your connection to your real self.

Your 'Real self' knows exactly how you can be successful in life! Once you're closely reconnected and reunited with your Higher self, that will unerringly assist and guide you ever step of the way to have the abundance and success your seek. This also includes guiding you to the fulfillment of your life's mission and purpose, which will offer you greater fulfillment and will give you a much meaningful life.

As you go on with your life's journey, getting rid of those limiting beliefs, you'll find a whole new life ahead of you – a changed life in so many wonderful ways! Yes, there is an actually lot of works that needs to be performed, but taking the right step at the right time will reward you with continuous prosperity, success, and abundance!

Real wealth does not just relate with your current financial situation. Real wealth definitely includes a spirit of gratitude and abundance for the real riches in life. That's what will make you really prosperous. This is how abundance really works in life.

CHAPTER 5

GETTING IN THE RIGHT MINDSET

Synopsis

The most important step that you should take in order for you to reach your absolute potential and achieve abundance in life actually begins with the right mindset.

There is lots of mindset that you can use, but among the most recommended and greatest is known to be abundance mentality. This mentality is the exact opposite of scarcity mentality.

Scarcity mentally is basically rooted from fear of having not enough things, and fear of losing.

Having this type of mindset, you are living your life under a false belief that supply, resource, lovers, and friends, are limited. This is definitely a sense of insecurity.

The Mindset

Abundance mentality, however, is rooted from confidence and positivity. With this, you strongly believe that resources are limitless for you to achieve the things you want in life. That life needs no worries, such worries about money. You can achieve this by believing that money is abundant in this world. You know that is an opportunity doesn't turns out good, there are still lots plenty of other opportunities out there waiting for you to discover. This will never affect you in such negative manner.

Those who are living with an abundance mentality, or those who have the right mindset don't fear difficult situations or obstacles, because even if things don't turn out according to what they want or what they plan, there are still lots of opportunities ahead of them – chances that can help them achieve abundance in the different aspect of their life.

Every person has this unique ability of manifesting all the things they want at will. Well, all you need to do is to have and equipped yourself with the right attitude and the right mindset. Here are some traits that you should possess to attract abundance in life.

- *Gratefulness*: There are lots of things that you should be grateful for regardless of your situation in life. Be thankful and appreciate all the little things, being grateful will attract more things into your life.

- *Belief*: Believe in yourself as well as in your ability of creating your own destiny and reality through your actions and thoughts. These are the keys to unlock your inner self and inner power. Self doubt can be harmful; it can even prevent you from achieving abundance and success in life.

- *Take action*: The universe always presents you with a lot of opportunities that will lead you straightly towards achieving your goals. Once opportunities are presented, take action. Don't wait for luck to do miracles for you, instead do your thing and make the right move.

- *Never force something to happen*: Learn to let go of things. Forcing some things to happen will makes matters worst – you being agitated and upset. There is always a reason why things happen. But even if it's true, you can also turn things the other way around because you have the power of doing so, which is superior that circumstances.

Well, getting the right mindset to achieve real abundance in life is the best thing to do. Life is supposed to be happy and joyful – love what you're doing, see to it that you real passion is potentially expressed.

Remember, that the power of attracting abundance is right within yourself and the right mindset.

CHAPTER 6

THE DIFFERENCE BETWEEN POSITIVE
AND NEGATIVE MINDSET IN ABUNDANCE

Synopsis

A positive mindset in life – the kind of focus that will help you attain abundance in life, achieve goals, overcome diversity, and realize all your potentials. But it doesn't mean that you have to avoid all the negative comments and thoughts.

Well, a positive mindset can give you the ability of feeling negative if you need to but still maintaining enough hope that can keep you going. You probably have heard about the saying that you have to change your negative mindset into a positive one, that you should avoid thinking or saying negative things. This is just an obvious denial of the things that make you human. A starting point to achieve abundance in life and create a much better life is for you to deeply understand the essence of being a human, and accept what and who you truly are. As human, you are imperfect, you are frail, and you are also a mistake prone being who can actually react emotionally to whatever things that happen to you.

Great Info

Negative Mindset Simply Means That You're Human

Life is full of challenges and obstacles that can turn to be disturbing, unsettling, and almost frightening. Most people will need to experience frustrations, struggles, and nightmarish situations at certain point of their life. This makes them stronger and tough – pushing them hard to achieve real abundance in life. Obstacles and challenges are normal in life and it is definitely okay for you to feel bad about it especially when things don't go according to your preference.

Yes a negative mindset can be misleading – but there are times when you need to have negative thoughts in mind especially when you path bends to a wrong way. But to deny all these thoughts and feelings simply would not be healthy and natural. It's about how you perceive this things, how you see them in having huge impact in achieving abundance in your life. Well, it is all about you. It is about how you handle things, how you weigh and balance your positive mindset over you negative mindset.

Don't worry yourself too much because of these negative thoughts and feeling that creep in your life. The most important thing to do is not allow these feelings hinder you from creating a better life and achieving abundance.

Positive Mindset Begins By Embracing The Reality

True positive mindset doesn't deny the reality or redo the history in order to make all things better that what they are. To completely and fully address the things that face you, you need to essentially and accurately define the things that you're dealing with. If you soften or minimize the true nature of your task, you will have the risks of not handling it with the needed amount of energy and importance.

Everything that will happen to you will offer you lessons that will help you navigate your journey. Regardless of how negative your current situation may seem, how bad you're feeling in this very moment, remember that wonderful lessons can be extracted from your journey and this will give you the wisdom that you need in order to create a much better world – a world full of abundance.

CHAPTER 7

HOW IMPORTANT IS FAITH?

Synopsis

Having lots of faith equals to having lots of abundance and prosperity in life.

It is essential for you to know how important it is to take steps that can increase and improve your faith. Faith opens doors to limitless resources, creative power, abundance, and success. No one actually can advance better and further in their life than their faith in God, themselves, and faith in achieving their goals in life. Faith will lead you to all great achievements. Without faith, you won't be able to achieve real abundance in life.

Faith

Your faith isn't just an empty fantasy, but it is a positive element. It's an absolute creative force that let you produce quantifiable things. "Now faith is the substance of things hoped for, the evidence of things not seen." – Hebrews 11:1.

Faith will lead you to great achievements, it doesn't think nor guess. It also sees and knows the best way out thus, a person who is supported by a strong faith will persist and will achieve the things they seek in life. It's through a strong faith that all greatest inventions and discoveries are made.

Missing faith in life towards God, yourself, and your purpose is one hindering factor to being successful and prosperous. Being human beings, some find it difficult to discover excellent possibilities and opportunities within themselves and establish faith needed for them to pursue and inspire their ambitions in life.

Increasing Your Faith And Unlocking The Power Within Yourself

From Romans 10:17, people are being told that their faith comes from hearing, especially hearing the 'Word of God'. It tells people that their faith comes not just by hearing once, but rather from hearing again and again. In addition to that, people need to hear the 'Word of God'. Though you can measure your faith in lots of aspects, but without a strong faith in the Word of God, you limit yourself.

The power and essence of faith in order for you to accomplish and to achieve is being emphasized. Christ said, "According to thy faith be it unto you." He emphasized two words – belief and faith above all other.

God created you for success, and not for failure. He definitely wants you to achieve the things you want and he wants you to prosper.

Thus, encourage yourself with great positive affirmations. Increase your faith and it will keep all your doubts away. Use strong faith for you to prosper and achieve abundance in the different aspects of your life.

CHAPTER 8

HOW TO ATTRACT EXACTLY WHAT YOU WANT?

Synopsis

Want to attract exactly the things that you want? Well, everything in this world is actually made up of energy – including you. And the first step that you should take to attract the things you want is to shift or change your energy.

People really pick up your energy. If it is positive, you will attract only positive things and positive people in your life. But if it is negative energy, you will always attract only negative situations and negative people right into your life.

If you think that you're getting the things that you don't like or that you're not getting the things that you really want in life, then there is a great possibility that you are sending off wrong energy.

Getting What You Want

To simply put it, you attract things that correspond and match your energy. Positive energy attracts positive situations and the other way around. It really is that simple. Thus, if you are not attracting the things that you want, you should shift your energy and you will start attracting exactly the things you want in life.

But what really is this energy? Well, you energy is something that is based from your beliefs and thoughts. Your own subconscious mind does pick up on the beliefs and thoughts you have in mind. It creates situations corresponding your beliefs and thoughts. In addition to that, other people also pick up on your energy as well and it's on their subconscious level. Meaning they are not basically and consciously aware about your energy yet they develop these feelings about your and based from your energy. Thus, if you actually have negative energy, chance is you will attract negative situations and negative people. And of course, you will repel all the positive situations and positive people.

How It Works?

If you think of worst things, if you're always negative, if you do not believe that you can achieve anything, if you always complain, if you see things in worst situations, if you always put other people down, if you are a totally negative person you will create a negative energy – at the end of the day, you will attract more negativity in life, allowing more negative people and situations in your life.

How Can You Turn Things The Other Way Around?

If you want to turn your negativity into a whole lot of positivity in life, you need to change how you see and perceive things. Start eliminating your negative beliefs and negative thoughts. This will definitely change the energy within you. With this, you will begin to attract the things you want the most.

This only means that you have to focus more on the positive situations, understand and believe that everything will turn out fine, look for solutions to your problems and stop complaining, transform yourself into a more understanding person, embrace the reality and the essence of change, and look for the opportunities and stop focusing on your problems. Stop believing the worst things will happen.

CHAPTER 9

ADVANTAGES AND DISADVANTAGES

Synopsis

Abundance is not something that you acquire; it is something that you work for. One of the most wonderful gifts that you can give yourself is the awareness and consciousness about the abundance and beauty in your life. This awareness will lead to a higher level of gratitude, and think of it as natural progression. Well, consciousness about abundance and gratitude are linked together inextricably.

The Good And Bad

The Advantages Of Having An Abundant Life

By meaning, abundance may mean plentiful. But it means fullness as well – fullness of the spirit and gratitude is the fullness. Well, if you are experiencing great abundance in life you should be thankful. The more you feel, think, and express your gratefulness:

The more you will attract and achieve things to be thankful for in your life.

The more you will become conscious or aware of how abundant your life really is.

The higher your gratitude will become, making your chakras, energy bodies, and therefore, your physical body healthier.

The Disadvantages

But the downside is that, some people by being prosperous, they tend to focus more on their happiness and tend to brag about their greatness.

They always feed their hungry ego, and this is one of the downsides of having an abundant life. Well, this is not true with all the people.

Some are being arrogant, instead of being thankful for what they have in life; they tend to seek for more not considering if they are affecting someone else.

Now, here is a challenge for everyone: Stop thinking and focusing about yourself, why not focus more on the interest and well being of other people? Isn't this a ways of being grateful for all the things you have in life, for achieving abundance and being prosperous?

Remember, self centeredness, self pity, and all the other form of selfishness will lead you to the path of misery.

If you really want a lasting happy and fulfilling life, then you should learn how to love and care for your fellow beings. Focusing on trying to make other people joyful and happy, you will become happier. Give and it will come back to you. It is actually an infinite and endless circle. Give and receive, it is a way of life.

Happiness or misery? Giving or self centeredness? What will you choose? Without love, people can't know real happiness. Without love, the door to spiritual happiness closes and the darkness envelopes people. Happiness is not about serving yourself or seeking material gains. You can experience abundance in love and happiness if you appreciate your life and what it has to offer.

CONCLUSION

Living your life abundantly starts from thinking abundantly. Prosperity and abundance is always available for anyone to obtain. For you to have more abundance in life, you have to begin by being aware and conscious about the abundance that you already have in life. You can't experience abundance only yesterday or even tomorrow, only at this moment of time that you can actually be aware about your richest blessings – your abundance in life.

Abundance doesn't start with material treasure or wealth, but they manifest with strong faith and with dedicated action. Consider abundance as a state of your mind, which arises from the feeling of gratefulness and gratitude for all the things that you have in life.

Whatever you want in life – contentment, peace of mind, inner awareness about simple abundance, it will definitely come to you. But this will only happen when you're ready to have it with a very grateful and open heart. Abundance doesn't occur by an opportunity or chance alone, it is from seizing your day as well as by accepting all the responsibility that will mold your future. It is seeing what people do not see, and pursue that vision.

In order for you to experience abundance in life, you should first decide and identify what abundance really means for you. Then you should see yourself as being already abundant. Most essentially, you should begin by giving to others in any way you can. You will eventually receive in multiples from the abundance that you bring to the life of other people.

Become aware and grateful for all the abundance around you – that brilliant sunset, the voice of your loved ones, your child's touch. Consider every breath and act of gratefulness and love as gifts – never take anything for granted.

Focus on the abundance you want to achieve in life. The way you want other people to treat you, the things that you want to have, the success and the things that often make you contented and happy. Realize that you can create them all by focusing on the things that you want in life. The universe will always be consistent, it responds to all your focus in life. Above all, appreciate all the things that you already have.

Abundant living comes when you live to give. Remember, one of the secrets of living abundantly is 'The Art Of Giving'. Don't let the spirit of fear hinders you from giving. You can actually give abundantly for you to live abundantly. Share. Consider abundance as an energy flow. Once abundance reaches you, don't keep it all to yourself instead share it to other people and make it flowing.

Printed by Libri Plureos GmbH in Hamburg, Germany